DINOSAUR WARS

TYRANNOSAURUS REX
★ ★ ★ ★ ★ ★
VS
VELOCIRAPTOR
★ ★ ★ ★ ★ ★ ★ ★ ★ ★ ★ ★ ★

POWER AGAINST SPEED

Michael O'Hearn

Consultant:
Mathew J. Wedel, PhD
Paleontologist

Raintree

www.raintreepublishers.co.uk
Visit our website to find out more information about Raintree books.

To order:
☎ Phone 0845 6044371
🖹 Fax +44 (0) 1865 312263
✉ Email myorders@raintreepublishers.co.uk

Customers from outside the UK please telephone +44 1865 312262

Raintree is an imprint of Capstone Global Library Limited, a company incorporated in England and Wales having its registered office at 7 Pilgrim Street, London, EC4V 6LB – Registered company number: 6695582

Editors: Aaron Sautter and Laura Knowles
Designer: Kyle Grenz
Media Researcher: Marcie Spence
Art Director: Nathan Gassman
Production Specialist: Laura Manthe
Illustrations by Philip Renne and Jon Hughes
Originated by Capstone Global Library Ltd
Printed and bound in China by South China Printing Company Ltd

ISBN 978 1 406 21821 3 (hardback)
14 13 12 11 10
10 9 8 7 6 5 4 3 2 1

ISBN 978 1 406 22089 6 (paperback)
15 14 13 12 11
10 9 8 7 6 5 4 3 2 1

British Library Cataloguing in Publication Data
A full catalogue record for this book is available from the British Library.

Acknowledgements
We would like to thank the following for permission to reproduce photographs: Shutterstock **parchment backgrounds** (Valery Potapova), **stylized backgrounds** (Leigh Prather).

CONTENTS

WELCOME TO DINOSAUR WARS!

Dinosaurs were brutal creatures. They fought each other and ate each other. Usually it was meat-eater versus plant-eater or big versus small. But in Dinosaur Wars, it's a free for all. Plant-eaters attack plant-eaters. Giants fight giants. And small dinosaurs gang up on huge opponents. In Dinosaur Wars, any dinosaur battle is possible!

In this dinosaur war, Tyrannosaurus rex and Velociraptor clash. You'll learn why these two hunters were feared. You'll discover their impressive weapons. You'll find out how fast they were and how they fought. Then you'll see them battling head-to-head – and you'll get to watch from a front row seat!

Tyrannosaurus rex (ti-RAN-oh-sore-us REX)
Velociraptor (vel-OSS-ih-rap-tor)

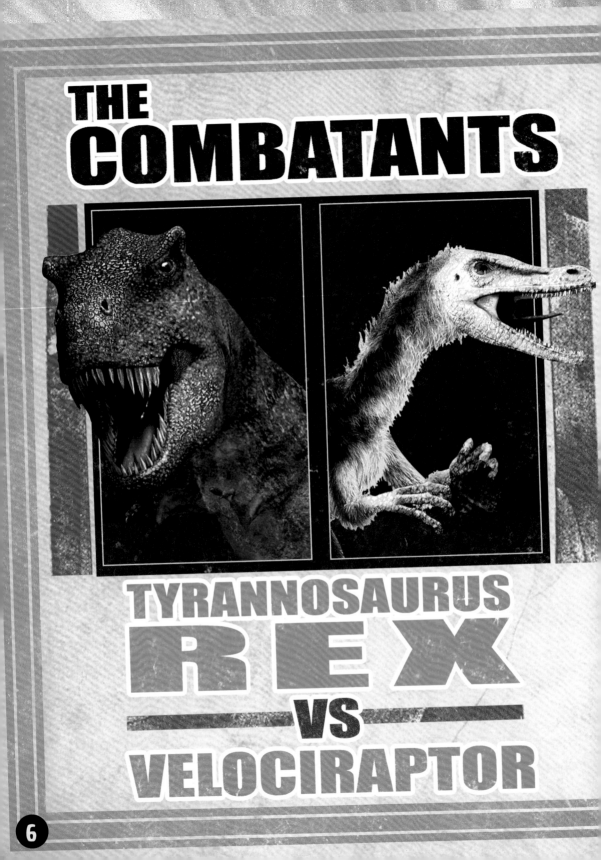

THE COMBATANTS

TYRANNOSAURUS REX
VS
VELOCIRAPTOR

Scientists know that a battle never happened between Velociraptor and Tyrannosaurus rex (also known as T. rex). Velociraptors lived about 80 to 84 million years ago. They died out more than 10 million years before the first T. rex ever lived, which was about 67 million years ago. T. rex lived until dinosaurs became **extinct** about 65 million years ago.

Even if Velociraptor and T. rex had lived at the same time, they made their homes on opposite sides of the planet. Velociraptor lived in Mongolia, which is near China. The first Velociraptor **fossils** were found in the Gobi Desert in Mongolia in 1922.

T. rex lived in the western United States and Canada. The first T. rex fossils were identified in the early 1900s. In the summer of 2000, a group of five T. rex skeletons was found in Montana, USA. Some scientists think one of these skeletons may be the largest T. rex ever found.

Most dinosaur skeletons in museums are missing some bones. Scientists fill in the gaps using models of bones from related dinosaurs.

FIERCE FACT
BONES

extinct no longer living anywhere in the world
fossil remains of an animal preserved as rock

SIZE

T. rex was a true heavyweight, big enough to take on any dinosaur. He was one of the largest **carnivores** to ever walk the earth. This monster stood 6 metres (20 feet) tall and weighed 6.4 tonnes. T. rex's head was massive. It was 1.4 metres (4.5 feet) long. T. rex could fit an entire Velociraptor inside his open mouth. Without question, T. rex had the size advantage.

carnivore animal that only eats meat

Velociraptor was puny compared to T. rex.
Velociraptor stood only about 1 metre (3 feet)
tall. He measured up to 1.8 metres (6 feet) long
from head to tail. Weighing just 16 kilograms
(35 pounds), Velociraptor was no heavyweight.
Compared to T. rex, he wasn't even a featherweight.

**T. rex was about 400 times
heavier than Velociraptor.
But this size difference might
be a hidden advantage for
the Velociraptor. For the
giant T. rex, Velociraptor
would be a small target and
difficult to catch.**

SPEED AND AGILITY

Velociraptor's small, light body and slim legs made him fast. Scientists think Velociraptor could run up to 39 kilometres (24 miles) per hour in short bursts. He could also make sudden, tight turns. His stiff tail stuck straight out behind him and helped him keep his balance when turning quickly. His speed and agility would be an advantage in a fight against T. rex.

Like Velociraptor, T. rex had a stiff tail for balance. But rather than helping T. rex turn quickly, it probably served to balance the weight of his giant head.

FIERCE FACT
THE TAIL

Some scientists believe T. rex could run just as fast as Velociraptor. But most others believe that T. rex was too big and bulky to run fast or turn quickly. T. rex might catch Velociraptor by surprise, but he probably couldn't chase down the speedy Velociraptor in a race.

WEAPONS

T. rex had 50 to 60 monstrous teeth. Some teeth grew more than 20 centimetres (8 inches) long. T. rex could bite down with more than 1,360 kilograms (3,000 pounds) of force. His powerful jaws and strong teeth could crush the bones of his **prey**. Any bone-crunching bite on a Velociraptor would cause serious damage or death.

prey animal that is hunted by another animal

To find the force of T. rex's bite, scientists studied fossils bitten by T. rex. They also performed experiments on cow bones using model T. rex teeth and mechanical jaws.

FIERCE FACT
THE BITE

Velociraptor didn't have T. rex's power. But with 80 sharp, curved teeth, he was skilled at holding on to his prey. His clawed hands were even better at gripping his enemies in a fight. However, Velociraptor's secret weapon was a large, hooked toe claw. He used it like a knife to slash at his prey. With it, he could wound even the mighty T. rex.

ATTACK STYLE

Tyrannosaurus rex
A powerful bite
★ ★ ★ ★ ★

TYRANNOSAURUS REX

T. rex's eyesight was perfect for hunting. His eyes were more forward-facing than the eyes of most other dinosaurs. This gave him good tracking vision. Sharp vision would be very helpful in a fight against the small and speedy Velociraptor.

T. rex was basically a big tank with teeth. His main attack move was to chomp down on his prey. His powerful jaws could easily overpower his victims. If his prey was large, he might drag it down or yank it off its feet. Some scientists think T. rex was also a scavenger, scaring off smaller meat-eating dinosaurs and eating their prey after they had done the hard work.

ATTACK STYLE

VELOCIRAPTOR

Velociraptor fought like a lion. He leapt on to the back of his prey and hung on tight with his front claws. After pulling down his prey, he slashed at his victim's throat and belly with his wicked toe claws.

Velociraptor may have hunted in packs. He certainly had the large brain and intelligence needed to hunt in packs. A pack of Velociraptors might have worked together like a pack of lions or wolves do today. Lions surround their prey so it has nowhere to escape. Wolves chase a victim towards a larger group of wolves for the kill. Fighting in a pack would be the only way Velociraptor could hope to defeat T. rex.

GET READY TO RUMBLE!

Are you ready for the pain? It's time for a serious dinosaur smack down. In one corner is one of the scariest creatures ever to walk the planet – T. rex! He's got bone-crunching teeth, a bad attitude, and he doesn't like losing. In the other corner is his opponent – Velociraptor! Fast and fierce, he attacks with nasty, sharp teeth and even nastier claws. He's small but **vicious**, and he has friends.

vicious fierce and dangerous

VELOCIRAPTOR

SIZE ★★★★★ / ★★

SPEED AND AGILITY ★★★★★★

WEAPONS ★★★ / ★★★★

ATTACK STYLE ★★★★★★★ / ★★★★★★

TYRANNOSAURUS REX

You've got a front row seat. So sit back, turn the page, and get ready to enjoy the battle!

ONE LAST THING...

This battle is fake. It's imaginary, like in a film. These two dinos never met or fought each other. Nobody knows which dinosaur would have won. No one knows how it would have happened. But if you like a good dinosaur battle, this one should be a blast!

THE BATTLE

T. rex is looking for a fight. Actually, he's looking for a bite. He's hungry for Triceratops or anything that looks tasty and meaty. But the pickings are slim. All he sees is a scrawny Velociraptor at the edge of a small lake.

Velociraptor doesn't seem concerned. He takes his time. He dips his mouth into the lake and gulps some water.

T. rex moves quickly towards the thirsty Velociraptor, who glances at T. rex but doesn't run. The **hulking** T. rex closes in on his tiny prey one thunderous step at a time.

Finally, when T. rex is only two steps away, Velociraptor comes to attention. He looks at the approaching monster, now within striking distance. T. rex opens his jaws and lurches forward. Velociraptor suddenly turns and bolts towards the trees. T. rex gets a mouthful of earth.

hulking large and heavy

Some dinosaurs, such as Velociraptor, had feathers like a bird.

Velociraptor is fast. He's out of reach before T. rex can spit out the soil. But Velociraptor doesn't get very far ahead. He glances back at the furious T. rex, who roars and charges.

Velociraptor zigzags and swerves in front of T. rex. T. rex's teeth crack loudly as his jaws snap shut just behind his intended victim. Velociraptor runs towards a large boulder next to some pine trees. He lets out a screech, leaps onto the rock, and then jumps over it. He disappears into the shadows.

FIERCE FACT HUNTING

Like today's predators, meat-eating dinosaurs had bigger brains than plant-eaters. It takes more brain power to hunt living creatures than it does to look for plants.

T. rex stops. He stares into the dark forest. It's silent and still. Suddenly, a screeching chorus erupts from the silence. A pack of Velociraptors bursts from the shadows. Before he can react, T. rex is covered with a dozen savage Velociraptors. The battle is on!

Using their sharp claws, the Velociraptors climb up on T. rex. They scurry up his tail and legs. Then they dig into his back, neck, and head. They bite with their many sharp teeth and slash with their dangerous toe claws.

T. rex's arms are too small to knock the tiny foes off his back. His long, stiff tail is also useless for swatting away the nasty creatures. T. rex roars and whips his huge head from side to side. The Velociraptors go flying. They land with a thud and tumble across the hard ground.

T. rex lunges forward and bites. Crunch! One Velociraptor disappears. Crunch! Another one is gone. Crunch! A third is chomped down in one bite.

FIERCE FACT
THE BITE

The force of a T. rex's bite is like having the weight of a pick-up truck pressing down on its prey.

The remaining Velociraptors continue slashing at T. rex. They open gashes in his scaly skin. They screech as T. rex roars. He keeps thrashing his head back and forth. But the Velociraptors hang on. They hack at T. rex's back and neck like crazed butchers. They kick fast and hard with their razor-sharp claws.

T. rex roars and shakes. Then he stumbles and slams into a tree. He scrapes his side across it to knock off his attackers. One Velociraptor loses its grip and drops to the ground.

T. rex lunges at the Velociraptor with his massive jaws. On its back, the fallen Velociraptor lashes out with all four limbs. He gouges T. rex's snout. The monster rears back and then dives again. This time, T. rex catches the Velociraptor and finishes the job. Crunch!

T. rex whips his neck and thrashes his body. He crashes through the trees, trying to knock off his opponents. But the remaining Velociraptors cling on tightly. T. rex jerks wildly and crashes to the ground. Two Velociraptors are crushed beneath him. The others are finally thrown off and slam into the ground. They bounce back up and rush at T. rex as he struggles to get up. The first one gets too close, and T. rex bites him in half.

T. rex rolls to his knees and finally climbs to his feet. He lunges at each of the remaining Velociraptors. They dodge his attacks and dart into the forest. They disappear among the shadows. Though cut and bloodied, T. rex is victorious. He lets out a wild roar to tell the world he's king of the dinosaurs!

The name Tyrannosaurus rex means "tyrant lizard king".

FIERCE
FACT
NAME

GLOSSARY

carnivore animal that eats only meat

extinct no longer living. An extinct animal is one whose kind has died out completely.

fossil remains or traces of plants and animals that are preserved as rock

herbivore animal that eats only plants

hulking large and heavy

massive very large, heavy, and solid

predator animal that hunts other animals for food. Tyrannosaurus rex and Velociraptor were predators.

prey animal hunted by another animal for food

tyrant cruel or unjust ruler

vicious fierce or dangerous

FIND OUT MORE

BOOKS

Dinosaur Encyclopedia, Caroline Bingham
(Dorling Kindersley, 2007)

Dinosaur Hunters: Palaeontologists, Louise and
Richard Spilsbury (Heinemann Library, 2007)

Prehistoric Scary Creatures, John Malam
(Book House, 2008)

WEBSITE

www.nhm.ac.uk/kids-only/dinosaurs
Visit the Natural History Museum's website to discover
more than 300 types of dinosaur, play dinosaur games,
and find out what sort of dinosaur you would be!

PLACES TO VISIT

Dinosaur Isle
Sandown, Isle of Wight PO36 8QA
www.dinosaurisle.com

Natural History Museum
London SW7 5BD
www.nhm.ac.uk

The Dinosaur Museum
Dorchester DT1 1EW
www.thedinosaurmuseum.com

INDEX